101 Diamonds

101 Diamonds

"*Mishkat al-Anwar*"
a collection of hadith by
MUHYIDDIN IBN AL-'ARABI

interpreted by
LEX HIXON / NUR AL-JERRAHI
and FARIHA FATIMA AL-JERRAHI

from the Oral Tradition of the
Glorious Messenger Muhammad

NEW YORK · PIR PRESS · 2002

Pir Press
227 West Broadway
New York, New York 10013

ISBN 1-879708-17-5

Printed in the United States of America

Calligraphy: "Muhammad, upon him be blessings and peace" by Mohamed Zakariya
Design: Peter Muller

May we each be blessed
to receive one of the 360 mystic glances
offered by Allah every day
to the loyal friends
of His gnostic saints.

NUR AL-JERRAHI

Contents

40 Khabar

21 Hadith

Acknowledgements

May Allah reveal the Truth to all those who helped in bringing this book about, and may they receive their inmost hearts' desires.

My parents, children, and extended family
Ali Rahman Karimnia, my companion
Haydar Friedrich
The family of Nur, especially his wife Sheila Hixon
Sixtina Friedrich
Matthew Brown
Ann Everds
Peter Muller
Pamela Mariam White
Mariam Nur Terwilliger
The dervishes of the Nur Ashki Jerrahi Community

Introduction

In the Name of Allah, the tenderly Merciful and
Infinitely Loving

This book is for every seeker of Truth. The guidance it offers transcends the boundaries of any particular historical tradition. It is the nectar of wisdom for the heart. Drink deep.

"Know your self and you will know your Lord."

May the sublime peace of Allah be showered upon the Prophet Muhammad who uttered these words of light 1400 years ago. They have guided countless Sufis on their return into Truth, and today they call countless more with their clarity and power. They tell the great secret that the path is through our own self—from the turbulent landscape of the narrow, limited self to the exalted heights of our illumined self—to our Lord Who is our very self; in this encounter we will disappear, for we have never truly existed as independent realities. The mirror melts, the cup breaks, the fire of Truth burns all that is not Itself. One Reality alone exists—there is no room for two. Our very essence is what we are seeking, and when we find it within, we no longer exist. Only He exists. This is the great knowing.

Yet how is it that we ardently desire intimacy and friendship with God if only God exists? If we have passed away in God why are we still longing for God? This is the eternal mystery of divine companionship—when we pass away from separate identity and illusory self, we live as God's light within God's light, the *Nurun ala Nur* as it is called in the mystic path of Islam. The primordial light of Allah reveals within Itself light upon light. The Self longs for Itself, and humanity is revealed in the outpouring of divine desire. We long for God and God longs for us. Only God can be with God.

LA ILAHA ILALLAH, THE SWIFTEST PATH TO TRUTH

This exalted state of Unity, although indescribable, is said by the mystic masters of Islam to be expressed in the divine Name—*La ilaha ilallah, Muhammad Rasulallah.* Supreme Reality Alone exists and reveals Itself as Perfect Humanity. Therefore sincere repetition and deep contemplation of this glorious sentence is the swiftest path to unveiling truth within the human heart. The Sufis are those who are constantly immersed in the divine Name.

Exalted companionship requires exalted behavior. Within the bridal chamber of the Sultan one acts differently than in the corridors of the palace or in the street. Therefore, our hearts seek knowledge of good behavior—knowledge of what is pleasing to Allah and what is displeasing, knowledge of how to behave as a true human being who is both servant and crown of creation. The holy Prophet stated that he was sent by Allah Most High to complete the knowledge of good behavior in humanity, and when he was asked about religion he responded simply that it is beautiful behavior. He prayed, "O precious Lord, increase me moment by moment in luminous knowing of You." His prayer is our prayer. Our longing for Allah expresses itself as the desire for deeper and deeper levels of intimate knowing pleasing to Allah.

THE HOLY QUR'AN AND ALL THE BOOKS OF REVELATION ARE THE MATRIX OF KNOWLEDGE

Revelation is the sharing of divinity with humanity—it is a divine gift which lifts human beings from a state of lostness, sadness and illusion to the station of reality and joy. Its essence is light, sheer radiance which takes the form of humanly intelligible yet extremely dense language. The perfect transparent receptive vessel, the Prophet Muhammad, may divine peace always embrace him, tells us that he received revelation in two ways. One was through the intermediary of the angel Gabriel, peace be upon him, who would appear to him and speak the holy words which the Prophet would then slowly repeat so as to seal them in his mind. The second way was through the ringing of a bell. The ringing sound would increase in intensity until it became almost unbearable, engulfing him. This audition was very difficult, and he was accustomed to cover himself with his cloak while his body trembled and perspired. In this reverberation the divine words manifested.

The language of revelation is not like our ordinary language, rather it is supercharged with infinite meanings. It is a primordial ocean of meaning, constituted of loving, creative power, and it requires interpreters who are trustworthy, people of honor whose hearts and minds have disappeared into Truth. The foremost interpreter of the revelation of Qur'an is the Prophet himself. Through the blessed example of his holy way of life and his verbal teachings, extensively recorded in Hadith, he unveils the infinite depths of the transcendent Qur'an.

THE MYSTICAL PATH: INITIATES OF THE WAY OF THE HEART

During his lifetime the Prophet Muhammad, may divine peace shower upon him, initiated a few of his companions and members of his close family into the mystic path, transmitting to them the most subtle teachings of Islam, the deepest meanings of Qur'an. The close ones who drank from this knowledge and then communicated it to others established the foundation of Sufism, and their way eventually became known as *Tariqat*—the inner path of the heart.

The Prophet's beloved daughter Fatima, with her noble husband 'Ali, received this initiation. Hazreti Fatima and Hazreti 'Ali, may their hearts be illumined with Allah's pleasure, were inheritors of the Prophet's knowledge and sublime behavior; and 'Ali is considered to be the source of the majority of mystical orders now existing. He is also responsible for many of the most important and longest hadiths. Yet after the passing of the Prophet from this world, it was Hazreti Fatima who embodied her father's light and was his first representative, the first *Khalif,* until her death six months later at the age of twenty-six. Her father would say of her: "Fatima is part of me." Therefore, the lineage of saints from the heart of the Prophet Muhammad, may Allah shower him with the nectar of radiant Peace, is first through Fatima. The lightening bolt of prophecy embeds itself in the breast of mercy, and from there spreads into the human family, where women and men together reveal the mysteries of Divine Reality. The station of Hazreti Fatima is particularly relevant to the West at this time when women are manifesting openly as spiritual guides.

THE MYSTIC KNOWLEDGE OF ABU HURAYRA

One of the companions of the Holy Prophet blessed with spiritual intimacy was Abu Hurayra, called "Father of the cats" because he cared for the stray cats in Medina. He was extremely poor as he preferred to spend as much time as possible in the presence of the Prophet, listening to his teachings, rather than seeking after his own livelihood.

Although he placed all his attention on the words spoken by the noble Messenger, he could not retain them in memory as he desired. One day he expressed his distress. The Prophet instructed him to spread his cloak and then made a gesture as if pouring something into it. From that moment, Abu Hurayra never forgot anything, and he became one of the most trusted transmitters of the traditions. In this collection he has contributed the greatest number of hadiths, and they are of a special mystical quality.

Abu Hurayra stated that the Prophet had imparted two degrees of knowledge to him. The first degree was for the entire community of practitioners, while the second degree, if shared, would bring about his execution by the same community. The second degree of knowledge relates to the Unity of Being, the fusion of human consciousness into Divine awareness, and to the all-embracing Mercy of Allah. Even among the close companions there was disagreement about the sharing of this kind of knowledge. One night in Medina, Abu Hurayra encountered the Prophet praying alone in a garden. The Prophet revealed to him that anyone who sincerely recited the mystic words *La ilaha ilallah* once in their lifetime would attain divine Forgiveness and eternal bliss. Abu Hurayra ran to share this extraordinary news with the other close ones. All of them were deeply imbued with the exalted principle of *La ilaha Ilallah Muhammad Rasulallah*, which embraces all levels of awareness. Yet, one of them upon hearing these words from Abu Hurayra, knocked him to the ground, exclaiming that he would not accept the message unless he heard it directly from the blessed lips of the Prophet. When the Prophet confirmed the statement, the companion begged him not to spread this knowledge as it could harm the very practice of religion. He feared many people would begin to rely on Allah's Mercy alone and become lax in their discipline, causing their downfall.

Since that time we have come to a different place in our spiritual evolution where we are actually seeking the essential teachings in all the spiritual traditions. In the heart of each path the Truth clearly speaks. So, like Abu Hurayra, we are the companions who would hasten to spread the news of the transformative power of *La ilaha Ilallah* and other holy mantras which are the essence of divine grace and self-knowledge. Both the urgency of the world condition and a new maturity of the heart makes the desire greater for this knowledge. As we experience the core of our own path it becomes apparent that One Truth is speaking through all paths of return. The implication of this new transparency is Love.

IBN AL-'ARABI'S COLLECTION OF 101 ORAL TRANSMISSIONS

Ibn al-'Arabi, the Greatest Shaykh as he came to be called, was born in the 12th Century in Islamic Spain. At a young age his outstanding intellect and luminous presence had attracted many of the living teachers and guides. Very early he himself became a guide for the Sufi community and a spiritual authority on Qur'an and Hadith. The doctors of theology, the *'ulama*, often found his radical interpretations, revealing the all-merciful nature of Allah, in contradiction to their own narrow point of view—and at certain times his life was in danger from the people of dogma. However, his stature as a spiritual giant protected him. The volume of Ibn al-'Arabi's writing was immense, creating a vast reservoir of mystic knowledge for all seekers of knowledge and practitioners of Sufism. At the age of twenty-five it was divinely revealed to him that he was the "Seal of Muhammadan Sainthood", "the Seal of Saints". He was the one who would reveal to the greatest degree the light of the Prophet Muhammad's heart and the hidden oceanic depths of his knowledge. Therefore he is the highest authority on the interpretation of Qur'an and Hadith after the Prophet and Hazreti 'Ali. This is why he came to be called the greatest of shaykhs, the teacher of shaykhs, *al-Shaykh al-Akbar.*

This present collection of texts, called *Mishkat al-Anwar,* was selected by Ibn al-'Arabi from the vast body of Hadith. Many of them he received from living transmitters, hearing some for the first time in the holy precincts of the noble Ka'ba. This collection of hadiths is not the only one he assembled, but it is said to be his favorite. He has arranged them in a way and a sequence which guides the reader on a path of learning: inducing awe, opening the heart, chastening, revealing and confirming the seeker, and finally immersing the seeker completely in Divine Mercy and Love. Selected as they are by the Shaykh al-Akbar, these hadiths present the highest teachings of Islam—they embody the essence of Islam. The soul is reminded of its high and beloved station as Truth, yet warned to remain uncompromisingly vigilant in this life regarding its hidden intentions, for subtle inner intentions are the only testimony accepted by Divine Reality. Allah Most High has stated "In evaluating the sincerity of your lives I will only take into account your hidden intentions, not your apparent actions." The balance of compassionate love and rigorous truth embodied in the teachings is the elixir needed to bring about the mature human being, the one ripened on the vine of tariqat—perfect humanity. This elixir is the knowledge of the Prophets, and there is nothing more precious than this knowledge.

TRANSMISSION FROM HEART TO HEART: A LINEAGE OF HOLY SAGES

The original transmissions of these 101 hadiths flowed directly from the Source of Being, calling itself Allah, into the heart of the Prophet Muhammad, may divine peace be always showered upon him as the perfect receptive vessel. They are called *Hadith Qudsi*, holy transmissions, because they are the direct words of the Holy One. Therefore their spiritual level and potency is very similar to Qur'an. As with each revelation he received, the Prophet immediately shared these teachings with his intimate companions, who recorded them in their hearts and shared them with others. After his passing from this world these companions were consulted on all important affairs and one of them would be chosen by the community to represent him. 'A'isha, the beloved wife of the Prophet Muhammad, was among those most consulted for her knowledge. Her noble husband had once said to her, "You will carry one third of my religion." As people came to her to inquire what the Prophet had related on certain subjects, her answers became part of the foundation of his way and they comprise about a third of all existing Hadith.

SHAYKH NUR AL-JERRAHI, A MODERN SAGE

In each time there are certain human beings entrusted with keeping the transmission of divine knowledge alive. They protect the creation through their light, and before leaving this world, they pass this role on to others. Lex Hixon, Shaykh Nur al-Jerrahi, the author of this English text, called these beings sages. He himself was one of them--a modern day sage. At all times, Nur affirmed the teaching that supreme Truth surpasses all conception and cannot be grasped, yet it is everywhere and is all that exists. The only way for seekers to realize truth is to unveil it within themselves, for they are never separate from it. Nur personally experienced Supreme Reality as boundless love, and he poured this wine of perfect love into countless open hearts. No amount of words can describe him or his means of teaching which were surprising, disarming, and compassionate. Whether he was called 'Shaykh Nur' or 'Lex' by the seekers of various paths who surrounded him, his life was always dedicated to revealing the true nature of the human spirit, and freeing the modern mind from the prison of materialism and existential doubt. He helped to liberate religion from the weight of compulsion, convention and patriarchy. He envisioned a humanity consistently inspired by the breath of divine love and continuously disappearing into divine Existence. He was a friend of all the great religious traditions, and worked for their mutual understanding and love. He never wanted to reduce one of these sacred worlds to the other, as he felt that each is a perfect expression of truth, and each has the potential to bring about complete realization.

For thirteen years, as a part of his relentless exploration and service, Lex conducted a radio program called *In the Spirit*. From this platform he interviewed spiritual teachers from all over the world, helping to draw an untold number of listeners into their own spiritual path. On one of the shows he met the living teacher who became his master and guide in the Sufi path. Shaykh Muzaffer Ozak al-Jerrahi was one who had become fully mature, a 'master of essence', the *Qutub* of his time. He embraced Lex as his spiritual son, and gave him the name Nur, divine light. Indeed Nur would manifest Islam as a dazzling path of light, truth and holy love. The lightning bolt had leapt from the East to the West.

Through the remaining fifteen years of his life Shaykh Nur Lex Hixon became a gushing spring of inspiration. Shaykh Muzaffer appointed him as the head of the community of American dervishes who gathered in the Masjid al-Farah in New York City. After the Shaykh's passing on February 12, 1985, many dervishes received mystic dreams of Nur as his successor, and so they took the pledge of the student to the teacher, the holy bond which is able to bring about complete spiritual realization in the heart of the aspirant. After the first transitional years, Nur's community began to grow and spread, particularly through his travels for book readings and his participation in spiritual gatherings. And so there formed a series of circles of lovers of God across the Americas, connected to the spiritual lineage of Shaykh Nur, Shaykh Muzaffer and the founding saint, Pir Nureddin Jerrahi.

Spiritual lineage is transmitted from heart to heart through the special relationship of teacher and student—the bond between one who embodies the light and the vessel who receives it in order to become a new embodiment. Spiritual transmission, formless and wordless, is likened to a ray of light leaping from the breast of the teacher into the heart of the student. This ray brings about a birth in the heart of the student called the *qalb weled*, the child of the heart. This child has the unique characteristics of its lineage. Following the guidance of the teacher and nourished with the light of Qur'an and Hadith, the child of light grows and matures until it too becomes a guide for others. This process brings about the formation and guarantees the continuation of spiritual community, which is the matrix of Sufism and the living embodiment of Qur'an and Hadith. In Islam, as in all the sacred traditions, knowledge becomes real when it is lived.

THE PROCEDURE OF UNVEILING IN THE
INTERPRETATION OF 101 DIAMONDS

When Shaykh Nur encountered *Mishkat al-Anwar* in its French version by Muhammad Valsan, he recognized the spiritual potency of these hadiths for contemporary humanity, and undertook his own inspired, interpretive translation. In his work, Nur relied both on scholarly translation and the method of inner unveiling, described in great detail by Ibn al-'Arabi as absolutely authentic and reliable. Unveiling is the divine revelation of truth within the heart which is open to God. It happens in a state of contemplative receptivity. When directed to passages of Qur'an and Hadith, the results can be quite different from a more scholarly approach, which is valid and helpful, yet remains in the realm of the rational. Nur contemplated each word of this holy text distinctly, allowing an essential meaning to come into his heart—he received a guided understanding of the essence of the hadith, and finally placed it within a beautiful, resonant form of English.

I began working with Shaykh Nur on this interpretation in 1993. In January of 1995, Nur learned of his illness—a cancer which was deemed inoperable by conventional medicine. At this time, we decided to work toward completing the editing process. During the next three months, I would meet with him in his light-filled living room, sitting by the large windows which opened onto gardens sloping down to the Hudson River. He would be dressed in a jogging suit or pajamas and his presence was intense and mother-like. As we immersed ourselves deeper into the book I began to wonder at some of the severity of the hadiths, and felt strongly that Nur should emphasize more the presence of mercy. For example, one of the hadiths portrays worshippers appearing on the Final Day before Allah, Who informs them that their lifetimes of worship and prayer add up to nothing because they were only seeking their own glory. And they are commanded to enter the chastening fire. I was uncomfortable for some time, until one night I received a dream in which Nur powerfully answered my dilemma. In the dream he stated that the hadiths embody a perfect spiritual balance between divine severity and divine mercy. The severity which I perceived was simply the sharpness of the sword of Truth whirling in the teachings. This intensity of truthfulness leaves no room for unclarity or doubt in our hearts. This is great mercy.

The living shaykh in the Islamic Sufi tradition is the representative of the Prophet Muhammad, and the transmitter, for his or her generation, of his Light—which has been passed mysteriously from saint to saint through 1411 years. The living shaykhs are the embodiment of Qur'an and Hadith—transcendent Book and oral tradition. They demonstrate and transmit this merciful guidance through their presence, their actions, and their words. The common book written by the human hand is a repository and presentation of wisdom teachings, but the most direct transmission occurs from heart to heart. This is the truest setting for receiving and assimilating Divine Revelation and following Divine Guidance. Through these pages, the reader may sense that they have subtly linked with a mystic community of hearts, receiving and participating in an authentic transmission of light. If so, this is because these hadiths have come alive through the heart of Shaykh Nur al-Jerrahi, so that the timeless wisdom of these 101 diamonds is manifested directly in our lives.

May his selfless service to the Truth be pleasing to Allah Most High, and may it be rewarded by bringing countless lovers into the Truth. May we all be included in his service, and may those who read this book be drawn into the highest levels of illumination.

Know your self and you will know your Lord.
The way is knowing.
Knowing is loving.
Loving is disappearing.
Disappearing is finding.
You are the essence.
You are the vessel.
You are the empty mirror.
Your Lord is the Outpouring, the Holy Face,
    the eternal I Am.
The noble Prophet Muhammad, the bringer of peace,
is the Heart.
He is the essential human divine form of Love, both
    and man and woman united as humanity.
He is the threshold between creation and essence.
He is the place of primal witnessing.
He is the supreme guide of return
    into the Source of Love.
In knowing our self we know that Divine Love is all.

Fariha Fatima al-Jerrahi

MARCH 15, 2002
MUHARRAM 1, 1423 A.H.
YONKERS, NEW YORK

101 Diamonds

Commentary

In the Name of Allah, the tenderly Merciful and
Infinitely Loving

MAY ALLAH MOST HIGH send His peace and blessings upon
our Master Muhammad, upon his blessed family and his noble
companions.

This servant, this poor *faqir* lost in the glory of Allah,
Muhammad ibn 'Ali ibn Muhammad Ibn al-'Arabi at-Tai al-
Hatimi al-Andalusi—may Allah seal his life with the highest
good—exclaims:

All praise flows to Allah, Lord of all the worlds. Felicity
belongs to those who are immersed in awe before Allah, and
there is no power and no strength except in Allah, the
Exalted, the Magnificent. May peace and blessings be showered upon Muhammad, master of the divine knowers, upon
the members of his pure household, upon his noble companions, upon his followers, and upon the entire community of believers.

According to the noble companion Ibn 'Abbas, the Messenger of Allah—may he be immersed in the highest peace—has declared: "The one who preserves and transmits to my community forty hadiths of my teaching will receive my intercession on the Day of Resurrection." According to Anas ibn Malik, the Messenger of Allah—may he be showered in divine peace—has also stated: "The one who preserves and transmits to my community forty essential hadiths will be inscribed by Allah Most High as one of the sages of Islam."

Imbued with this perfect counsel of the Prophet—divine peace be upon him—and concerned more with the Hereafter than with this world, I have gathered these forty hadiths in Mecca—may Allah Most High protect her—during the year 599. I selected only those hadiths revealed directly by Allah the Exalted. These are followed by forty more, also divinely revealed, but lacking the chain of transmission from the Prophet of Allah, may he be showered in luminous peace. I will complete the selection with twenty-one more *hadith qudsi* in order to reach the definitive total of 101.

May Allah Most High grant us knowledge which is beneficial to us and to you, and may He place us among those who belong entirely to Him, through His exalted grace and His loving favor. His sublime power mercifully extends over all creation.

40 Hadith

O MY CHERISHED SERVANTS

Muhammad the Messenger, may Allah bless him and grant him peace, once transmitted these words directly from the Most High:

O cherished servants, as I have made injustice unlawful for Me, so I have made it unlawful for you. Be not unjust.

O servants, all of you are wandering astray except the ones whom I have guided. Ask Me to guide and I will guide you.

O servants, all of you are hungry except those whom I have fed. Ask Me to feed you and I will feed you.

O servants, all of you are naked except those whom I have clothed. Ask Me to clothe you and I will clothe you.

O servants, indeed you are erring night and day, yet I forgive all offences. Ask Me to forgive and I will forgive you.

O servants, although you may think you are doing harm to Me through your negative actions, no harm can reach Me. Although you may imagine you are benefitting Me through your good deeds, these acts of yours cannot add the least particle of goodness to My Own overflowing Goodness.

O servants, even if the entire spectrum of intelligent beings—from the first of you to the last of you, from human beings to beings on subtle planes—possessed the heart of the most evolved ones among you, this would add nothing to My Kingdom.

O servants, even if all intelligent beings, from first to last, possessed the heart of the most rebellious ones among you, this would take away nothing from My Kingdom.

O servants, if all intelligent beings, visible and invisible, gathered together and demanded their most sublime wishes from Me and I granted every one of them, this would in no way diminish the treasures that are with Me, any more than a needle dipped in the ocean would decrease the ocean.

O servants, I take account of your deeds only according to their subtle inner intentions, and it is according to these intentions that I will fully reward you.

O servants, those who see goodness all around them are opening their entire being to the praise of Allah. Those who find other than the good can blame only themselves.

◆ This hadith comes from the transmission of the noble companion Abu Dharr, may Allah be pleased with him.

Hadith ◆ 2

THE ONE BEYOND ALL EQUAL

Muhammad the Messenger, may Allah bless him and give him peace, once transmitted these words directly from the Most High:

I am the One beyond equal, free from any reality other than My Reality. Therefore, those who pledge their devotion and worship to any other than Me are not with Me, and belong instead to that illusion which they chose over Me.

◆ This hadith comes from the transmission of the intimate companion Abu Hurayra, may Allah be pleased with him.

Hadith ♦ *3*

THE SECRET LOVERS

Muhammad the Messenger, may Allah bestow grace and peace upon him, once transmitted these words directly from the Most High:

> *Among the most intimate to Me of My saints are the believers of humble means who find their pleasure in prayer, worshiping their Lord in the most beautiful way, and who obey Him both secretly and openly. These saints are hidden among the people. They are not always pointed out by Me. They are content with small sustenance. They receive and bear trials patiently.*

The Messenger of Allah went on to comment about these secret lovers:

> Their death comes swiftly, their mourners are few, their family inheritance is meager.

At that, he struck his thigh with great enthusiasm.

♦ This hadith comes from the transmission of the noble companion Abu Umama, may Allah be pleased with him.

Hadith ✦ 4

ACCUSER AND ACCUSED

While the glorious Messenger, upon him be peace, was seated among his companions, they saw him smile so widely that his eyeteeth were revealed. Omar the Just inquired: "Why are you smiling, O Messenger, more precious to me than my father and mother?" The noble Prophet responded:

Two believers will one day kneel before the Lord of Power, may He be exalted. The accuser will pray: "O Lord, grant me compensation for the harm this brother has inflicted upon me."

Allah Most High will address the accused: *Offer spiritual compensation to your brother for the harm you have caused him.*

The accused will announce: "O Lord, I have not a single good deed left to offer him."

"Then let him carry some of my burdens," the accuser will pray.

The eyes of the Messenger, may Allah bless him and grant him peace, filled with tears, and he interjected:

That will truly be a terrible day when human beings will need someone else to carry their burdens.

The noble Prophet continued:

Allah, may He be glorified and magnified, will then address the accuser: *Raise your eyes and gaze into the Gardens of Paradise.*

He will lift his head and exclaim: "O Lord, I see cities of silver and palaces of gold crowned with pearls. To what prophet or martyr do these beautiful abodes belong?"

They belong to the ones who pay Me the full price.

"O Lord, who is able to do that?"

You are able to do that.

"How, O Lord?"

By forgiving your brother.

"O my Lord, I forgive him instantly."

The Most High will continue: *Now take the hand of your brother, and allow him to enter Paradise.*

The Messenger, may Divine Peace be upon him, then remarked:

Be in loving awe of Allah Most High and make peace among yourselves, for then Allah will establish His Own Peace among you on the Day of Resurrection.

◆ This hadith comes from the transmission of the noble companion Anas ibn Malik, may Allah be pleased with him.

PARADISE AND HELL

Muhammad the Messenger, may Divine Peace be upon him, once revealed:

Upon creating Paradise and Hell, Allah sends Archangel Gabriel to Paradise, saying: *Go look upon it and upon all the abundant gifts I have prepared for its inhabitants.*

The Archangel travels there, looks upon Paradise and upon the wonders that Allah prepared. On returning, Gabriel exclaims: "By Your Loving Power, no one will even hear of Paradise without instantly and ardently seeking it." Allah Most High then ordains that Paradise be veiled by difficult tasks and sends Gabriel once more. Upon returning from beholding what Allah prepared, the Archangel exclaims: "By Your Loving Power, now I fear that no one will be capable of entering Paradise."

Allah proclaims to His Archangel: *Go forth to visit the Fire and look upon it and upon all I have prepared for its inhabitants.*

The noble Gabriel observes great tumult and confusion. He returns to his Lord and exclaims: "By Your Loving Power, whoever even hears of the Fire will not wish to enter it." Allah then ordains that Hell be surrounded by attractive desires and passions and sends Gabriel once more. The Archangel returns, exclaiming: "By Your Loving

Power, I now fear that no one will be able to resist the Fire."

◆ This Hadith comes from the transmission of the intimate companion Abu Hurayra, may Allah be pleased with him.

Hadith ◆ 6

RECITE ONCE THE SURA FATIHA

Muhammad the Messenger, may Divine Peace be upon him, once reported these words spoken by Allah Most High to Archangel Israfil, upon him be peace:

By My Loving Power, by My Majesty, by My Overflowing Generosity, by My Nobility! Concerning those who cry out "bismillahi-r-rahmani-r-rahim, in the Name of Allah Most Compassionate, Most Merciful," and then recite once the opening chapter of Holy Quran, Sura Fatiha, be you witness, O Israfil, I have already forgiven these persons. I have accepted their acts of goodness and separated them from their acts of negation. I will not place the Fire upon their tongues. I will protect them from the Divine Chastening experienced after death by those who lead lives of negation. I will save them from great terror on the Day of Resurrection. I promise they will meet Me directly in the blessed company of all prophets and saints.

◆ This hadith comes from the transmission of the great companion Abu Bakr the Truthful, may Allah be pleased with him.

Hadith ♦ 7

THE ONE REALITY

Muhammad the Messenger, may Divine Peace be upon him, reported these words directly from the Most High:

Some children of Adam slander Me by claiming that I have given birth to a son. Others accuse Me of falsely promising eternal life to the soul, insisting, "Allah cannot call me to eternal life as He called me to earthly life." Eternal resurrection is no more difficult for Me than earthly creation. As for the slander "Allah has begotten a son," I am the One, the Complete. I do not give birth, and neither was I born. There is nothing apart from Me, the One Reality.

♦ This hadith comes from the transmission of the intimate companion Abu Hurayra, may Allah be pleased with him.

TRULY FAITHFUL

Prophet Muhammad, may Divine Peace be upon him, reported these words directly from the Most High:

O children of Adam, only by remembering and contemplating Me with your whole being are you truly faithful to Me. Whenever you forget Me, you are unfaithful.

◆ This hadith comes from the transmission of the intimate companion Abu Hurayra, may Allah be pleased with him.

Hadith ◆ 9

MY HAND OF ABUNDANCE

The noble Messenger, may Divine Peace be upon him, reported these words directly from the Most High:

Spend generously for others from the spiritual and material means I provide you, and I will spend generously for you from My Divine Provision. My Hand of Abundance is always full. No spending, even if it continues night and day, will ever diminish My Abundance.

Muhammad the Messenger, upon him be peace, then added:

Have you contemplated what Allah, may He be exalted and glorified, has expended since He first created the heavens and the earth? This outpouring has not in the least decreased what He holds in His Hand. His Throne rests upon the primordial waters, and He holds the Balance, which on the Day of Judgment will weigh the minutest intentions behind every action performed by His servants.

◆ This hadith comes from the transmission of the intimate companion Abu Hurayra, may Allah be pleased with him.

Hadith ◆ 10

WHEN THEIR LIPS ARE MOVING
FOR THE SAKE OF ME

The Messenger of Allah, may peace be upon him, directly received these Divine Words:

I am with My servants when they remember Me, when their lips are moving for the sake of Me.

◆ This hadith comes from the transmission of the intimate companion Abu Hurayra and is confirmed also by the noble companion Mother Umm ad-Darda, may Allah be pleased with them.

Hadith ◆ 11

I HAVE NOT MADE POSSIBLE

The beloved Prophet, may Allah grant him peace and blessings, once reported these words directly from the Most High:

I have not made possible in the hearts of My servants the co-existence of two kinds of fear and two forms of security. If they remain in profound awe of Me in this world, they will not fear Me in the next world. If they become complacent about Me in this world, there will be no security for them in the next.

◆ This hadith comes from the transmission of the noble companion 'Abd-Allah ibn 'Umar, may Allah be pleased with him.

Hadith ◆ 12

ON THIS MAGNIFICENT DAY

The beloved Messenger, may Divine Peace be upon him, once received these words, which will be spoken by Allah Most High on the Day of Resurrection:

Where are those who love each other simply for the sake of My Splendor? I wish to cover them with My Shade, on this magnificent Day when there is no shade other than My Shade.

◆ This hadith comes from the transmission of the intimate companion Abu Hurayra, may Allah be pleased with him.

Hadith ◆ 13

I AM WITH MY SERVANTS

Muhammad the Messenger, may Divine Peace be upon him, once reported these words directly from Allah Most High:

I will appear to My servants at the End of Time in the way in which each expects Me to appear. Yet I am with My servants invisibly, even now, whenever they call upon Me.

◆ This hadith comes from the transmission of the intimate companion Abu Hurayra, may Allah be pleased with him.

Hadith ✦ 14

ASSOCIATE NOTHING WITH ME

The beloved Prophet, may peace be upon him, once revealed:

Allah Most High will ask those among the people of the Fire who are experiencing the mildest chastening: *If you now possessed all that is on earth, would you give it to redeem yourself?*

"Yes, precious Lord."

Yet I asked of you something much easier while you were still in the earthly form of Adam—that you associate nothing with Me in your worship of Me. You avoided every other error, but you did not avoid the error of regarding other powers as equal to Me.

✦ This hadith comes from the transmission of the noble companion Anas, may Allah be pleased with him.

Hadith ◆ 15

MY MYSTERIOUS ROBES

Muhammad the Messenger, may Divine Peace be upon him, once reported these words directly from Allah Most High:

My mysterious robes are Transcendence and Magnificence. Whoever contends with Me for one of these will encounter the Fire.

◆ This hadith comes from the transmission of the intimate companion Abu Hurayra, may Allah be pleased with him.

Hadith ◆ 16

I WILL NEVER NEED TO CHASTEN YOU AGAIN

The beloved Messenger, may Divine Peace be upon him, once reported these words, which Allah Most Glorious will speak on the Day of Resurrection:

The angels have interceded, the prophets have interceded, the believers have interceded. Now the Most Merciful of the Merciful will intercede. He will draw out from the Fire even persons who never offered acts of goodness and whose hardened hearts will have already been melted into lava. He will then immerse them in the river that flows before the entrance to Paradise called the River of Life.

Now enter My Paradise. Whatever you see there will be yours.

"Our Lord, You have bestowed forgiveness upon us which You have not given to anyone else in all the universes."

There is with Me something much more precious for you.

"O Lord, what could be more precious than what we see before us?"

My eternal Good Pleasure is upon you. I will never need to chasten you again.

◆ This hadith comes from the transmission of the noble companion Abu Sa'id, may Allah be pleased with him.

Hadith ◆ 17

GENEROSITY AND NOBILITY

Muhammad the Messenger, may Divine Peace be upon him, once received these words of Allah from Archangel Gabriel:

Behold, here is the religion that I accept as My very Own. Only generosity and nobility of spirit are suited to it. Honor it always with generous and noble thoughts and actions.

◆ This hadith comes from the transmission of the noble companion Jabir ibn 'Abd-Allah, may Allah be pleased with him.

Hadith ◆ 18

DIRECT VISION OF THEIR LORD

Muhammad the Messenger, may Allah bestow blessing and peace upon him, once revealed:

When the destined companions of Paradise enter Paradise, Allah the Exalted will inquire: *Do you wish Me to add something further to the bounties you now possess?*

They will reply: "O Lord, have You not already illumined our faces and hearts with Your purest Light? Have You not invited us into Your Paradise and guarded us from the Fire?"

Allah will then raise the veil from before His Countenance. This direct vision of their Lord, may He be exalted and glorified, will be infinitely more precious than the gifts of Paradise already bestowed upon them.

Thereupon the Messenger, may peace be upon him, recited this noble verse from the glorious Quran:

"Those who live beautiful lives of goodness are promised Divine Goodness, and even more."

◆ This hadith comes from the transmission of the noble companion Suhayb, may Allah be pleased with him.

HALF THE PEOPLE OF PARADISE

The beloved Prophet, may Allah bestow blessing and peace upon him, once revealed:

On the Day of Resurrection, Allah will call: *O Adam!*

Adam will respond: "I am here at Your Command, O Lord."

Separate from your posterity the group destined for the Fire.

"O Lord, who is destined for the Fire?"

For every thousand, there can be as many as 999 so destined. On the Last Day, pregnant wombs will abort, hair of children turn white, and human beings wander as though drunk. Such is My terrible Chastening.

These Divine Words had such impact on the companions who were listening that the very structures of their faces were changed. Observing this, the Prophet, may Allah's Peace be upon him, explained:

From the people of Gog and Magog, there will be 999 from every thousand who are destined for Divine Chastening, yet from my blessed community there will be only one from every thousand so destined. My community will shine forth from humanity like the black hairs on the side of a white bull or the white hairs on the side of a black bull. My community will represent at least a fourth of the inhabitants of Paradise."

Upon hearing this wonderful news, the companions cried out in joy the affirmation of Divine Greatness, *allahu akbar.* Then the glorious Messenger, upon him be peace, further revealed:

At least a third of the people of Paradise.

The companions cried *allahu akbar* again. The beloved one revealed once more:

At least half the people of Paradise.

The companions cried *allahu akbar* again and again.

◆ This hadith comes from the transmission of the noble companion Abu Sa'id al-Khudri, may Allah be pleased with him.

Hadith ◆ 20

CONTENTMENT WITH MY DIVINE DECREE

Muhammad the Messenger, may Divine Peace be upon him, conveyed these words of Allah first revealed to His beloved Prophet Moses:

Nothing that brings you close to Me do I love more than your contentment with My Divine Decree. You can do nothing that will preserve your acts of goodness better than being content to concentrate on your own responsibility. O Moses, do not seek support from the people of this world, for this will alienate you from Me. Do not compromise with this world in any way that is contrary to true religion, for this will close the doors of My Mercy to you. Moses, say to those who are constantly turning to Me, "Rejoice, O believers." And say to those who humble themselves before Me, "O believers, continue always to abstain from evil and to practice goodness."

◆ This hadith comes from the transmission of the noble companion Ibn 'Abbas, may Allah be pleased with him.

Hadith ◆ *21*

WHAT NO MIND HAS EVER CONCEIVED

Muhammad the Messenger, may Divine Peace be upon him, once conveyed these words directly from Allah Most High:

For My righteous servants, I have prepared what no eye has ever seen, what no ear has ever heard, and what no mind has ever conceived.

◆ This hadith comes from the transmission of the intimate companion Abu Hurayra, may Allah be pleased with him.

Hadith ◆ 22

THOSE WHO HAVE NOT KNOWN ME

The chosen Messenger, upon him be peace, once conveyed these words directly from Allah Most High:

Those who place their hope in any other than Me have not truly known Me. Those who have not known Me have not truly worshiped Me. Those who have not worshiped Me encounter My Displeasure. Therefore, those who stand in awe of any other than Me have brought My Displeasure upon themselves.

◆ This hadith comes from the transmission of the sublime companion ʿAli ibn abu Talib, may his countenance be illumined.

Hadith ♦ 23

YOU WILL HAVE ALL THIS
AND INFINITELY MORE

The chosen Messenger, upon him be peace, once received this revelation concerning the Day of Resurrection:

A certain soul will remain with its face toward the Fire. It will be the last among those to enter Paradise. This soul will cry out: "O Lord, turn my face away from the Fire, for its acrid odor tortures me and its heat consumes me." The soul will continue supplicating Allah in this way as long as the One Reality wishes.

Then Allah, may He be exalted, will inquire: *If I respond to your supplication, will you request anything more of Me?*

"No, Lord, I will not ask for anything more." Thereupon the soul will make whatever promises and vows Allah Most High desires. Allah will then turn its face away from the Fire. Upon beholding the light of Paradise, the soul will remain silent for as long as the One Reality wishes and then cry out: "O Lord, please allow me to advance to the Gates of Paradise."

Allah, may He be exalted, will reply: *Did you not promise that you would ask for nothing more? Alas for you, O child of Adam, how easily you break your vow.*

The soul will plead, "O Lord," continuing to supplicate Allah, exalted and glorified is He, until He responds.

And will you request anything more of Me if I grant you this?

"No, O Lord. By Your Loving Power, I will ask for nothing more." Acting as the Divine Will ordains, this soul will swear and promise. Allah will then permit it to advance to the Gates of Paradise. Clearly observing Paradise overflowing with goodness and delight stretched out before its gaze, the soul will remain silent as long as Allah wills and then will supplicate: "O Lord, please permit me to enter Your Paradise."

Did you not swear and promise that you would ask nothing further of Me? Alas for you, O child of Adam, how easily you break your vow.

"O Lord, please do not make me the most miserable of Your creatures."

The soul will not cease pleading in this way until Allah is filled with Good Pleasure. When Allah manifests this Divine Good Pleasure, He will intimately address the soul: *Now enter My Paradise.*

Thereupon Allah, may He be glorified, will address the soul in Paradise: *Make further supplication to Me.*

The soul will then ask for many sublime gifts, which Allah Most High will inspire it fervently to desire, reminding the soul of this or that aspiration, until all its longing is fulfilled.

Allah the Exalted will then declare: *You will have all this and infinitely more.*

◆ This hadith comes from the transmission of the intimate companion Abu Hurayra, may Allah be pleased with him.

Hadith ◆ 24

PEACE BE UPON YOU

Muhammad the Messenger, may Allah grant him abundant blessings and peace, once revealed:

When Allah Most High created Adam and breathed His merciful Spirit into him, Adam sneezed and called out: *"Alhamdulillah,* all life praises only Allah." By Divine Permission, Adam continued to praise ceaselessly.

His Lord responded: *My Mercy and Love are upon you, O Adam! Go now to the gatherings where the angels are seated and greet them with the words "salaam alaykum," peace be upon you.*

The angels responded to Adam: "And may the Peace and Mercy of Allah be also upon you."

The noble father of humanity returned to his Lord, who revealed: *This shall be the greeting and response among your descendants throughout time.*

Then Allah mystically unveiled His two Divine Hands: *Choose one of them, O Adam.*

"I choose the Right Hand of my Lord, even though both His Hands are one blessed Right Hand."

Allah then opened His Divine Hand, revealing to Adam his vast posterity.

"O Lord, who are all these human beings?"

These are your descendants, O Adam.

The destined life span of each was inscribed on the fore-head between the eyes. Among them was a person shining with a bright light, among the brightest of all. Adam asked: "O Lord, who is this?"

He is your descendant David, to whom I have given forty years of life.

"O Lord, please lengthen his life."

These years are what I have divinely appointed for him.

"O Lord, give him sixty years of my life."

That is your free decision, O Adam.

Adam dwelt in Paradise as long as Allah ordained and then left Paradise, as Allah also ordained. While living on earth, Adam kept count of his years. When Israfil, the Angel of Death, came to him, Adam cried out: "You are sixty years early. I was given a thousand years."

"True, but you gave sixty of your years to your descendant David."

Adam forgot his vow and denied the Angel of Death. Following this event, the posterity of Adam also became forgetful of their vows. Since that day, human beings are divinely commanded to rely upon documents and witnesses.

◆ This hadith comes from the transmission of the intimate companion Abu Hurayra, may Allah be pleased with him.

THE CHILDREN OF ADAM WHO
GIVE WHOLEHEARTEDLY

Muhammad the Messenger, may Divine Peace be upon him,
once recounted:

When Allah created the earth, it began to tremble, so He
created the great mountains to anchor it. Thereby the
earth was balanced.

Amazed by the power of these mountains, the angels inquired: "O Lord, is there anything in Your Creation more
powerful than these primordial mountains?"

Yes. Iron is more powerful.

"Is there anything in Your Creation, O Lord, more powerful than iron?"

Yes. Fire is more powerful.

"Is there anything in Your Creation, O Lord, more powerful than fire?"

Yes. Water is more powerful.

"Is there anything in Your Creation, O Lord, more powerful than water?"

Yes. Wind is more powerful.

"Is there anything in Your Creation, O Lord, more powerful than wind?"

Yes. The children of Adam who give wholeheartedly from the right hand, unknown to the left hand.

◆ This hadith is from the transmission of the noble companion Anas ibn Malik, may Allah be pleased with him.

Hadith ♦ 26

WHOEVER HAS ADORED ME

Muhammad the Messenger, may Allah bless him and give him peace, once clarified the nature of the Day of Judgment:

There will be a certain community composed of immature believers. Allah Most High will manifest Himself to them in an aspect other than the one they know and will say to them: *Behold, I am your Lord. Follow Me.*

"We take refuge in Allah from you," they will answer. "We will not move from here until our Lord, may He be exalted and glorified, comes to meet us. When our Lord appears, we will recognize him instantly."

Allah the Exalted will then come to them in the aspect which they expect and will proclaim: *Behold, I am your Lord.*

They will cry out, "You are our Lord indeed," and will follow Him.

When the bridge that crosses safely over the Fire manifests, Allah will proclaim: *Whoever has adored Me in even one of My infinite aspects should now follow Me confidently with that particular understanding.*

♦ This hadith comes from the transmission of the intimate companion Abu Hurayra, may Allah be pleased with him.

Hadith ♦ 27

I AM WITH THE BELIEVERS

Muhammad the Messenger, may Divine Blessing and Grace be upon him, reported these words directly from Allah Most High:

I am with the believers however they may remember Me and repeat My Names. If they remember Me silently within the heart, I remember them within My Heart. If they remember Me in gatherings, I remember them in a far more exalted gathering. If they come close to Me by as much as the width of a hand, I come close to them by an arm's length. If they come close to Me by an arm's length, I come close to them by two arm's lengths. If they come toward Me at the speed of walking, I approach them at the speed of running.

♦ This hadith comes from the transmission of the intimate companion Abu Hurayra, may Allah be pleased with him.

Hadith ◆ 28

AS LONG AS YOU INVOKE ONLY ME

Muhammad the Messenger, may Divine Peace be upon him, reported these words directly from Allah Most High:

O children of Adam, as long as you invoke only Me, pray only to Me, and place all your hope only in Me, I will forgive you whatever you have done, and I will not consider it any further. O children of Adam, even if your errors reached as high as the clouds in the sky and yet you asked for My forgiveness, I would forgive you. O children of Adam, if you came to Me with as many sins as the earth could hold and yet would meet Me without recognizing any other source of power, I would meet you with an equal amount of forgiveness.

◆ This hadith comes from the transmission of the noble companion Anas ibn Malik, may Allah be pleased with him.

Hadith ✦ *29*

AFTER A NIGHT RAINFALL

Muhammad the Messenger, may Allah bestow Divine Peace upon him, performed the dawn prayer at Hudaybiya after a night rainfall. As he completed the prostrations, he turned toward the people and asked:

Do you know what your Lord proclaims?

Those present answered: "Allah and His Messenger alone truly know."

The beloved Muhammad, upon him be peace, then revealed these words directly from the Most High:

This morning among My servants certain ones have believed in Me and others have not. Those who thought "It rained by the Grace and Mercy of Allah" believed in Me and renounced the stars. Those who thought "It rained because of a certain star" have renounced Me unknowingly and believed instead in the power of the stars.

✦ This hadith comes from the transmission of the noble companion Zayd ibn Khalid al-Juhani, may Allah be pleased with him.

Hadith ◆ *30*

ALLAH HEARS THE ONE WHO PRAISES HIM

Muhammad the Messenger, may Allah bless him and grant him peace, once explained:

> When the leader of the prayer intones, *Allah hears the one who praises Him,* you should call in response, *O Lord, all praise belongs only to You.* Allah, may He be exalted, will certainly hear you, because He originally proclaimed this phrase, *Allah hears the one who praises Him,* through the mouth of His Prophet.

◆ This hadith comes from the transmission of the noble companion Abu Musa al-Ash'ari, may Allah be pleased with him.

Hadith ◆ 31

THEY WILL RECEIVE INFINITELY MORE
THAN THEY ASK FOR

The glorious Messenger, may Divine Peace be upon him, once transmitted these words directly from Allah Most High:

I have apportioned the opening Sura of the Glorious Quran between Me and My servants: their act of praising and My Response to their praise. When My servants affirm, "All praises flow to Allah, Lord of countless worlds," Allah the Exalted responds: "My servants have praised Me." When the servants affirm, "the Most Merciful, the Most Loving," Allah responds: "My servants have intensely praised Me." When they affirm, "Sovereign of the Day of Judgment," Allah responds: "My servants have glorified Me and taken complete refuge in Me." When they affirm, "You alone do we worship and from You alone do we seek help," Allah responds: "This level of praise remains a secret between Me and each of My servants, and they will truly receive what they ask for." When they pray, "Guide us on the straight path, the path of those upon whom You shower Your Favor, not the path of those who incur Divine Correction," Allah responds: "This level of praise belongs to My most intimate servants, and they will receive infinitely more than they ask."

◆ This hadith comes from the transmission of the intimate companion Abu Hurayra, may Allah be pleased with him.

Hadith ◆ 32

A SECRET KNOWN ONLY UNTO ME

A companion questioned Muhammad the Messenger, may Allah bless him and give him peace, about the meaning of the Quranic Sura Ikhlas. The beloved Messenger replied:

I once posed this very question to Archangel Gabriel, who supplicated the Lord of Power concerning Ikhlas and received these words from Allah: *Ikhlas is a secret known only unto Me. I entrust it to the hearts of those whom I love most intensely among My servants.*

◆ This hadith comes from the transmission of the noble companion Hudhafiya, may Allah be pleased with him.

Hadith ◆ 33

FOR THE SAKE OF MY MAJESTY

The glorious Messenger, may Allah bless him and shower peace upon him, revealed these words directly from the Most High:

Those who love each other here simply for the sake of My Majesty will there receive thrones of light that will amaze even prophets and martyrs.

◆ This hadith comes from the transmission of the noble companion Mu'adh ibn Jabal, may Allah be pleased with him.

Hadith ◆ *34*

EYES THAT CAN ALREADY SEE PARADISE

The beloved Messenger, upon him be Divine Peace, once revealed these words directly from Allah Most High:

Whenever I deprive My servants of their two eyes in this earthly world, they receive from Me nothing less than eyes that can already see Paradise.

◆ This hadith is from the transmission of the noble companion Anas ibn Malik, may Allah be pleased with him.

I SWEAR UPON MY OWN SELF

The glorious Messenger, may Divine Peace be upon him, once revealed:

> There will emerge in the final days teachers who will use religion to deceive humanity. They will clothe themselves before the eyes of the people in the fleece of tender sheep. Their tongues will seem to flow with honey. Yet their hearts will be those of wolves. Allah Most High will ask the souls in nearness to Him: *Are these false teachers unconscious of Me, or are they trying to provoke Me? I swear upon My Own Self, I will bring on them a chastening that will leave even the most brilliant among them bewildered.*

✦ This hadith comes from the transmission of the intimate companion Abu Hurayra, may Allah be pleased with him.

Hadith ♦ 36

I BESTOWED UPON YOU ALL GOOD THINGS

Muhammad the Messenger, may Allah immerse him in peace, once revealed:

On the Day of Resurrection, the descendants of Adam will be brought like lambs before Allah, who will say to them: *I bestowed upon you all good things, including spiritual gifts and graces. What have you done with them?*

Some will answer: "We gathered them all together, we made them fruitful, and they became more abundant. Allow us to return to earth, and we will show them to You."

Allah will reply: *You must demonstrate true abundance to Me here and now, or else you will be directed to the Fire.*

♦ This hadith comes from the transmission of the noble companion Anas, may Allah be pleased with him.

Hadith ♦ 37

THE GATE OF THE RIGHT HAND

Muhammad the Messenger, may Allah immerse him in peace, once revealed these words concerning the Day of Resurrection:

I will cry out to Allah in the prayer of intercession: "My community, O Lord! My people, O Lord! All humanity, O Lord!"

Allah Most High will respond: *O beloved Muhammad, among the Gates of Paradise, bring those of your people whose lives have been fully clarified through the Gate of the Right Hand. They will also be empowered to enter all the other beautiful Gates of Paradise with all the other blessed souls.*

♦ This hadith is from the transmission of the intimate companion Abu Hurayra, may Allah be pleased with him.

Hadith ◆ 38

THIS PROMISE FROM ALLAH MOST HIGH

As I entered the Mosque in Medina, I saw the Messenger, may Allah immerse him in peace, coming forth from the house of prayer. I followed him, without his appearing to notice my presence. He entered a palm grove, turned in the direction of prayer, and prostrated. He prolonged his prostration to such an extent, while I stood quietly behind, that I thought Allah had taken his soul. I approached very close to him and bent down to see his face. Soon afterward, he raised his head, asking, "What is it, 'Abd-ar-Rahman?"

"O Messenger of Allah, your prostration was so prolonged I feared that Allah All-Magnificent and All-Glorious had taken your soul. I came close to see.":

O my companion, when you observed me entering the palm grove, I had just encountered Archangel Gabriel, upon him be peace, who brought me this promise from Allah Most High: *O beloved Muhammad, to those who send you greetings of peace, I offer My Peace. To those who call down My Blessing upon you, I send the same blessing.*

◆ This hadith comes from the transmission of the noble companion 'Abd-ar-Rahman ibn 'Awf, may Allah be pleased with him.

Hadith ◆ 39

I WILL PROTECT YOU FROM THE
FEAR OF POVERTY

Muhammad the Messenger, may Divine Peace embrace him, once conveyed these words directly from Allah Most High:

O children of Adam, give your entire being to the worship of Me. I will fill your heart with riches, and I will protect you from the fear of poverty. If you do not immerse your being completely in Me, I will fill your hands with the vain labors that can never protect you from the fear of poverty.

◆ This hadith comes from the transmission of the intimate companion Abu Hurayra, may Allah be pleased with him.

Hadith ◆ *40*

THOSE WHO MAKE ANY OF THESE
AFFIRMATIONS

Muhammad the Messenger, may Allah surround him with peace, once revealed:

Whoever testifies, *la ilaha ilallah,* there is nothing apart from Allah, and *allahu akbar,* Allah is greater than any conception, is approved by the Lord of Power, who responds to the soul: *In truth, there is nothing apart from Me, and I certainly transcend all conceptions.*

If the human witness testifies, "There are no powers apart from Allah, the One and Only," Divine Reality responds: *In truth, there are no powers apart from Me, the One and Only.*

If the soul proclaims, "There are no separate sources of being apart from Allah, the One and Only, who has no partner in the act of creation," the Lord responds: *In truth, there are no separate sources of being apart from Me, the One and Only, for I have no partners in creation.*

If the witness affirms, "There are no separate sources of being apart from Allah, and to Him alone belongs the Kingdom, and to Him alone flows all praise," Allah Most High responds: *In truth, there are no separate sources of being apart from Me, and Mine is the Kingdom, and all praises flow only to Me.*

If the worshiper prays, "There are no separate sources of being apart from Allah, and there is no power or strength except in Allah," the All-Merciful One responds: *In truth, there are no separate sources of being apart from Me, and there is no power or strength except in Me.*

The Messenger of Allah, may peace be upon him, then continued:

Those who make any of these affirmations at the moment of death will never be touched by the Fire.

◆ This hadith comes from the transmissions of both the noble companions Abu Sa'id al-Khudri and Abu Hurayra, may Allah be pleased with them.

THIS SERVANT, this poor faqir lost in the Glory of Allah, Muhammad ibn 'Ali ibn Muhammad ibn al-'Arabi—may Allah erase his faults, those of his parents, his sisters and brothers, and his companions, and the errors of the entire community of Muslims and all humanity—calls out upon completing these forty oral traditions: The forty Hadith are now fully transmitted according to what was promised! May Allah Most High grant ease and help through them!

I have presented these revealed words, along with their authentic lineages of transmission, which go back directly to Allah Most High. Most of the traditions I have collected came to me through my spiritual companions on the way, who received them in turn from their beloved masters and guides. It is appropriate that these masters be acknowledged here as belonging to the sublime rank of the sages of Islam, who transmit not only the letter but the true spirit of the oral traditions of the Messenger, upon him be peace. I will now present forty oral traditions without including their lineages of transmission, words which can be traced directly to Allah Most High.

40 Khabar

bismillahi-r-rahmani-r-rahim
In the Name of Allah, the tenderly Merciful
and Infinitely Loving

O Lord, open the way for these transmissions,
through the blessing of Your noble Prophet, upon him be peace.

EVEN A SINGLE MOMENT OF FORGETFULNESS

Allah the Glorious and Majestic inquires of his intimate friend the noble Prophet Abraham, upon him be peace: *Why such apprehension?* Abraham replies:

O Lord, why should I not experience profound apprehension? My spiritual father Adam was in the station of nearness to You. You created him with Your Own Hand and breathed into him Your Own Spirit. You commanded the angels to bow down before him. Yet for a single act of forgetfulness, You exiled him from Your Direct Presence.

Allah Most High then speaks into the secret heart of His friend:

O Abraham, do you not know that even a single moment of forgetfulness of the lover for the Beloved is terrible?

◆ This khabar was transmitted through the sage Ibrahim ibn 'Abd-Allah.

THE HEART THAT IS OBSESSED

Allah Most High proclaims:

O My Prophet David, warn the children of Israel against their obsessions, for the heart that is obsessed veils its own natural perception of Me.

◆ This khabar was transmitted through the sage Abu Ja'far al-Jazari.

I AM THE INTIMATE FRIEND

The noble Moses, upon him be peace, inquires:

O Lord, if You are distant, I will call out to You; if You are near, I will confide in You with intimate tones.

Allah Most High answers:

I am the intimate Friend of the persons who practice Divine Remembrance by repeating My Name, and I always keep company with them.

What is the act of devotion You prefer over all others, O Lord?

That you extend the repetition of My Name into every conscious state.

◆ This khabar was transmitted through the sage al-Maqburi.

MY TRUE LOVERS

Allah the Glorious and Majestic proclaims:

He speaks falsely who claims to love Me yet neglects Me for even a moment. Does not the true lover desire continuous intimacy with the beloved? I well know My true lovers, who behold Me ceaselessly. They adore Me during deep states of contemplation and converse with Me while immersed in My Presence during daily life. Tomorrow, I will refresh their eyes in My Gardens of Paradise.

◆ This khabar was transmitted through the sage al-Mufaddal.

TO THOSE SERVANTS MY PARADISE IS VEILED

Concerning those who take their own lives, Allah Most High reveals:

To those servants who have attempted to determine the career of their own souls, My Paradise is veiled.

◆ This khabar is found in the collection of the sage Muslim, along with its lineage to the Prophet, upon him be peace.

Khabar ◆ 46

REPEATING MY NAME EVEN WHEN IN BATTLE

Allah the Glorious and Magnificent proclaims:

My true servants are those who remember Me by repeating My Name even when in battle, face to face with the enemy.

◆ This khabar is found in the collection of the sage at-Tirmidhi, along with its lineage to the Prophet, upon him be peace.

Khabar ◆ *47*

BE FREE ON THAT DAY FROM DISTRESS
AND REMORSE

Allah Most High proclaims:

O children of Adam, if you could see the minute span of precious time that remains until your death, you would renounce all selfish projects and vain expectations. You would restrain your desire to possess, in all its subtle forms. And you would wholeheartedly seek to intensify your good actions. Otherwise, regret will seize you as you are falling into death, when your family and servants leave you, when friends distance themselves from you and even intimates abandon you. From the moment of death, you will no longer be able to return to your people or increase your good actions. Therefore, live now with a clear vision of the Day of Resurrection and be free on that Day from distress and remorse.

◆ This khabar was transmitted through the sage Wahb ibn Munabbih.

BRING YOUR HEART AND YOUR BODY
INTO PEACE AND HARMONY

Allah the Exalted proclaims:

O children of Adam, if you are truly pleased with the life-experience I have decreed for you, this will bring your heart and your body into peace and harmony and you will become praiseworthy. If you are not satisfied with your portion, I will subject you to this earthly world so completely that you will run back and forth like a wild animal deep in the desert. I swear by My Omnipotence and by My Majesty, you can gain nothing more beautiful than what I have already decreed for you. To ignore this would be blameworthy.

◆ This khabar was transmitted through the sage Ka'b al-Ahbar.

PEACE BE WITH YOU FOREVER

Allah Most High will proclaim to the people of Paradise as they enter Paradise:

My Peace is upon you, O beloved servants. Welcome to My Divine Ease. May you be filled with My Divine Life. As-salaam alaykum. Peace be with you forever.

◆ This khabar was reported by the sage an-Naqqash, along with its lineage to the Prophet, upon him be peace.

O HUMANITY, YOU ARE UNJUST TO ME

Allah the Exalted proclaims:

O sons and daughters of Adam, persons desire you only for themselves. I alone desire you truly for yourselves, yet you flee from My Countenance. O humanity, you are unjust to Me.

◆ This khabar was transmitted through the sage Ka'b al-Ahbar.

NO MISFORTUNE OR ADVERSITY
BUT YOUR MERCY ALONE

Before plunging them into the Fire, Allah Most High will say to those who have commanded and dominated in the earthly world:

O children of Adam, have you ever experienced any pure goodness, any pure delight?

They will answer: "No, O Lord."

Before embracing them into Paradise, the Glorious One will say to those who have been commanded and dominated in the earthly world:

O children of Adam, have you experienced any misfortune, any adversity?

They will answer: "No, O Lord! All praise to Allah, we have experienced no misfortune or adversity but Your Mercy only."

♦ This khabar is found in the collection of the sage Muslim, along with its lineage to the Prophet, upon him be peace.

Khabar ◆ 52

THE BREAD OF YOUR SUSTENANCE

Allah the Sublime and Magnificent proclaims:

O children of Adam, I created your physical forms from dust and sperm, and this creation was effortless. What difficulty can there be for Me to bring the bread of your sustenance before you at the proper moment?

◆ This khabar was transmitted through the sage Ka'b al-Ahbar.

Khabar ◆ 53

THE NEARNESS OF THE MOST GENEROUS ONE

Allah the Exalted will proclaim at the End of Time:

Peace be upon you from the Most Compassionate, the Most Merciful, the One Who is Life, the One Who is Self-Manifesting. You are the blessed ones. Enter now into the perfect contentment of Paradise. Delight in everlasting bliss, the nearness of the Most Generous One, the eternal abiding.

◆ This khabar was reported by the sage an-Naqqash, along with its lineage to the Prophet, upon him be peace.

Khabar ◆ 54

THROUGH MY UTTER COMMITMENT TO YOU

Allah the Sublime and Magnificent proclaims:

O children of Adam, I love you through My utter Commitment to you. You can love Me also only through My Commitment to you.

◆ This khabar was transmitted through the sage Ka'b al-Ahbar.

Khabar ◆ 55

YOU ARE THE FAITHFUL ONES

Allah the All-loving will proclaim to the people of Paradise:

You are the faithful ones, and I am Allah the Faithful and the Protector of the Faithful. I have dedicated to you, O faithful ones, My Divine Name, Mumin, the Faithful. You will never again be fearful, nor will you grieve. You are My friends, My close ones, My honored ones, My chosen ones, My intimate ones, My beloved ones. And you will dwell forever in My Abode.

◆ This khabar was reported by the sage an-Naqqash, along with its lineage to the Prophet, upon him be peace.

THE LAST THIRD OF THE NIGHT

Allah, may He be glorified and magnified, draws mysteriously near during the last third of the night and reveals:

I am Supreme Sovereign. To those who pray to Me now at this silent time, I respond. To those who ask from Me now, I give. Those who seek My forgiveness now, I forgive.

◆ This khabar appears in the collection of the sage Muslim, along with its lineage to the Prophet, upon him be peace.

BEAUTIFUL ACTION

Allah, All-Compassionate and All-Merciful promises:

If My servant sincerely intends a beautiful action, I record it before it is accomplished. If it is actually completed, I record it as ten beautiful actions. If My servant intends a negative action, I forgive it as long as it is not accomplished. If it is committed, I record only one negative action.

◆ This khabar appears in the collection of the sage Muslim, along with its lineage to the Prophet, upon him be peace.

Khabar ◆ 58

I HAVE CREATED YOU FOR MY DELIGHT

Allah, may He be exalted and glorified, proclaims:

O children of Adam, I have created you for My Delight, and I have brought forth the creation for your pleasure. Therefore, do not corrupt what I have created for Myself with what I have created for you.

◆ This khabar appears in the collection of the sage ar-Raba'i.

THE SUSTENANCE I WILL BRING YOU
TOMORROW

Allah the Sublime and Majestic proclaims:

O children of Adam, just as I never inquire about your ac-
tions of tomorrow, never question Me about the sustenance I
will bring you tomorrow.

◆ This khabar appears in the collection of the sage ar-Raba'i.

I AM PEACE

Allah the Exalted and Magnificent will confirm to the people of Paradise:

Peace be upon you, O assembly of My submitted servants. You are the peaceful ones, and I am Peace. My Abode is the Abode of Peace. Now I will unveil My Countenance to you, as clearly as on earth I revealed My Word.

◆ This khabar is part of the Oral Tradition reported by the sage an-Naqqash.

I NEVER FAIL IN MY OBLIGATION

Allah the Sublime and Majestic proclaims:

O children of Adam, you owe Me remembrance, and I owe you sustenance. Even if you fail in your obligation, no matter what your action, I never fail in My obligation.

◆ This khabar was transmitted by the sage Ka'b al-Ahbar and appears in the collection of the sage ar-Raba'i.

Khabar ◆ 62

I WILL PRESERVE YOU

Allah, may He be exalted and glorified, proclaims:

O children of Adam, pray four cycles of prostration at the day's dawning, and I will preserve you until the day's completion.

◆ This khabar is transmitted by the sage an-Nasa'i, along with its lineage to the Prophet, upon him be peace.

I ALONE HAVE CREATED YOU

Allah the Sublime and Majestic proclaims:

O children of Adam, how can you deny My Power? I alone have created you, fashioning for you a beautiful and harmonious form. Yet you begin to move about arrogantly, causing the earth to tremble beneath your steps. You begin to amass wealth without sharing it, until your soul reaches your throat at the moment of death and you cry out to Me: "Now I wish to give in charity." How can you imagine this last moment to be the proper time to establish your intention?

◆ This khabar is part of the Oral Tradition transmitted by the sage Asad ibn Musa.

I AM NEVER AN UNJUST LORD

Allah, may He be exalted and glorified, reveals:

If My servants lose their state of ritual purity and do not per-
form fresh ablutions, they are unjust toward Me. If they per-
form the rite of ablution without offering two cycles of prostration,
they are unjust toward Me. If they offer prostrations without
concluding by supplicating Me, they are unjust toward Me.
If they have made clear supplication and have waited with-
out receiving any response from Me, then I would be unjust
toward them. But I am never an unjust Lord.

◆ This khabar was transmitted by the noble companion Ibn al-Jarrah,
may Allah be pleased with him.

Khabar ◆ 65

IT WILL REMAIN FULL ETERNALLY

Allah the Sublime and Majestic proclaims:

O children of Adam, never fear lack of sustenance as long as My Treasury is full, and it will remain full eternally.

◆ This khabar appears in the collection of the sage ar-Raba'i.

YOU WILL NEVER BE VEILED FROM ME AGAIN

Allah, may He be exalted and magnified, will address the people of Paradise:

I now manifest to you by unveiling My Essential Face. Praise Me and enter My Abode in perfect peace and perfect certainty. You will never be veiled from Me again.

◆ This khabar is part of the Oral Tradition reported by the sage an-Naqqash.

Khabar ◆ 67

MY POWER ABIDES ETERNALLY

Allah the Exalted and Magnificent proclaims:

O children of Adam, never be afraid in any way of one who possesses limited powers as long as My Power abides, and My Power abides eternally.

◆ This khabar appears in the collection of the sage ar-Raba'i.

THE BRIDGE INTO ETERNITY

Allah the Sublime and Glorious proclaims:

*O children of Adam, do not imagine yourselves to be exempt
from trials and tests, as long as you have not crossed over
Sirat, the bridge into eternity. Only people who have lost their
way imagine that they are beyond the trials that come from
Allah All-Merciful.*

◆ This khabar appears in the collection of the sage ar-Raba'i.

I DELIGHT YOU WITH MY FAVOR

Allah Most High will address the people of Paradise:

Now return to Me and gather near Me so that you may behold Me and experience Me as I really am. I grant you My Graces. I delight you with My Favor. I envelop you in My Light. I clothe you with My Beauty. And I give you each a portion of My Kingdom.

◆ This khabar appears in the Oral Tradition reported by the sage an-Naqqash.

Khabar ♦ 70

I RESPOND PROFOUNDLY TO THE PRAYER

Allah Most Sublime reveals:

I respond profoundly to the prayer of those who humble them-selves before My Splendor, those who do not seek domination over My creatures, those who do not spend their nights per-sisting in disobedience toward Me, those who consecrate their days to constant remembrance of My Divine Names, those who are merciful toward the poor, the wayfarer, the widow, and every suffering person. The light of such supplicants ra-diates like the sun. I protect them with My Power, and My an-gels are also their protectors. In the darkness, I give them light. When they are surrounded by the ignorance of the world, I give them knowledge. Among My creatures, these supplicants shine forth as the highest Paradise shines forth in eternity.

♦ This khabar appears in the collection of the sage al-Bazzar.

IF THEY REFRAIN FOR MY SAKE

When the angels say, "O Lord, these servants of Yours are intending to perform a negative action," Allah the Exalted and Glorious responds:

Observe these servants. If they actually perform the negative action, inscribe in their books only one negative action. If they refrain, inscribe for these servants a good action, but only if they refrain for My Sake.

◆ This khabar appears in the collection of the sage al-Baghawi.

Khabar ◆ 72

ONLY THROUGH DIVINE GENEROSITY

On the Day of Resurrection during the evaluation of actions, Allah Most Exalted will command the angels:

Examine the daily prayers of My servants and see if they were performed partially or completely. If performed completely, they will be inscribed as such. If only partially, look to see if My servants have offered prayers in addition to the basic prayers that I have required. Complete with these additional prayers the partial prayers of My servants.

After speaking these words from Allah, Muhammad the Messenger, upon him be peace, commented:

It is only through Divine Generosity that any of our good actions are accepted.

◆ This khabar I, Ibn al-'Arabi, received orally from the contemporary sage who composed the *Book of Prayer.)*

POVERTY, SICKNESS, DEATH

Allah the Exalted and Glorified proclaims:

O children of Adam, I have given you three burdens: poverty, sickness, death. Despite the humbling power of these gifts, however, you remain bent upon your own aggrandizement.

◆ This khabar was transmitted by the sage Musa ibn Muhammad, along with its lineage to the Prophet, upon him be peace.

Khabar ◆ 74

AS LONG AS YOU HAVE NOT HEARD

Allah Most High revealed to the noble Moses, may peace be upon him:

I will teach you five truths that are the pillars of universal religion. As long as you have not heard that My Kingdom has ceased, do not abandon obedience to Me. As long as you have not learned that My Treasures are exhausted, do not be concerned about your sustenance. As long as you have not heard that the enemy of humanity has been defeated, do not feel exempt from surprise attack and do not cease to oppose Satan. As long as you have not heard that I have forgiven all your actions of past, present, and future, do not be critical of My other servants. As long as you have not yet entered My Paradise, do not feel that My testing of you has come to an end.

◆ This khabar was reported by the sage Yunus, relying on the sage Janir, who provided its lineage to the Prophet, upon him be peace.

A SERVANT PROPHET OR A PROPHET KING

Allah the Exalted and Magnificent once offered this choice to the beloved Muhammad, upon him be peace:

Is it your preference to be a Servant Prophet or a Prophet King?

Archangel Gabriel witnessed the humility of the glorious Messenger, who instantly responded:

I prefer to be a Servant Prophet.

◆ This khabar appears in the collection of the sage Isma'il al-Harawi.

MY INTIMATE FRIENDS

Allah, may He be exalted and glorified, proclaims: *Whoever humiliates one of My intimate friends directly challenges Me.*

◆ This khabar appears in the collection of the sage Isma'il al-Harawi.

SINCERELY OFFERING RIGHT GUIDANCE

Allah Most High proclaims:

The act of worship that I love most is sincerely offering right guidance.

♦ This khabar appears in the collection of the sage Isma'il al-Harawi.

Khabar ◆ 78

ASK FROM ME

Allah, may He be exalted and glorified, will proclaim to the people of Paradise:

I am your Lord, whom you worshiped and adored on earth without seeing Me directly, bringing before Me the desires of your heart, loving Me and standing in awe before Me. By My Power, My Majesty, My Sublimity, My Greatness, My Splendor, and My Radiance, I am pleased with you, I love you, and I love what you love and those whom you love. Whatever your souls desire and whatever delights your eyes is with Me alone. You have in Me all you long for and all you need. Whatever you desire, I desire also. Ask from Me, and be free forever from fear and grief.

◆ This khabar appears in the collection of the sage an-Naqqash.

I AM TIME

Allah Most High proclaims:

The children of Adam misunderstand Me when they complain against Time, for I am Time. In My Hand is the Command. I alone cause the day of knowledge to follow the night of ignorance.

◆ This khabar appears in the collection of the sage al-Bukhari, along with its lineage to the Prophet, upon him be peace.

Khabar ♦ 80

I HAVE ALREADY FORGIVEN THEM

On the blessed day each year that the pilgrims gather upon the plain of Arafa, Allah the Exalted commands the angels:

Behold My servants. They have come to Me from all directions, weary, covered with dust. I take you as witnesses that I have already forgiven these pilgrims.

The angels respond: "O Lord, this person has been unjust, as has this one and that one." Allah Most High affirms:

I have already forgiven them.

♦ This khabar appears in the collection of the sage Qasim ibn Asba.

THIS SERVANT, this poor one who lives only in Allah, calls out with gratitude. These forty transmissions, originating from Allah, to Him be glory and exaltation, are now completed! These Khabar appear without detailed historical lineages. We will now follow them with twenty Hadith, Oral Traditions presented with their historical transmission, originating in Allah, flowing through the Prophet of Allah, upon him be peace, and witnessed by the noble companions, may Allah be pleased with them.

I intend the present collection to comprise one hundred selections from the glorious Oral Tradition, which contain the direct words of Allah Most High. I will add one more, to insure an uneven number because, as the Most High reveals, Allah is uniquely single and therefore loves odd numbers.

21 Hadith

bismillahi-r-rahmani-r-rahim
In the Name of Allah, the tenderly Merciful
and Infinitely Loving

May Allah grant Mystic Union and Divine Peace
to our master Muhammad, to his beautiful family and
to his noble companions.

Hadith ✦ 81

LONG ARDENTLY TO FIGHT IN
THE WAY OF ALLAH

Muhammad the Messenger, upon him be Divine Peace, reported these words from Allah Most High concerning those who leave home to fight for the protection of the religion:

I send My noble warriors forth with the pure intention of fighting in My Way, experiencing complete faith in Me and acknowledging all My Prophets. After giving these warriors the vision of a reward never offered before, I assure them that they will either enter Paradise as martyrs or return safely to their homes.

Thereupon the Messenger, upon him be peace, proclaimed:

By the One who holds the soul of Muhammad in His Hand, there are no persons wounded along the Way of Allah, exalted be He, who do not appear on the Day of Resurrection in the very state of valor in which their wounds were received. The complexion of these noble warriors will be bright as blood and their scent sweet as musk. By the One who holds the soul of Muhammad in His Hand, if it were not for the distress felt by unarmed Muslims, I would never stay in the rear of any battle waged for the sake of Allah. I do not have the means to equip all Muslims for battle, nor do they themselves have the means, and it would be intolerable for them to be left behind, far from me. Therefore, I stand with them. By the One who holds the soul of Muhammad in His Hand, were it possible, I would long ardently to fight in the Way of Allah, to be martyred, to fight again and be martyred, and to fight again and be martyred again.

◆ This hadith, appearing in the collection of the sage Muslim, was originally reported by the intimate companion Abu Hurayra, may Allah be pleased with him.

Hadith ◆ 82

BURNING WITH DESIRE AND LOVE

Muhammad the Messenger, may Allah grant him perfect peace, once said:

Our Lord, blessed and exalted is He, revealed to me His Divine Good Pleasure concerning a faithful believer who was doing battle in the Way of Allah. His warrior companions were scattered. Fully aware that he was without their protection, he returned and fought bravely until his blood was spilled. Thereupon the Exalted and Majestic One proclaimed to His angels: *Look upon My servant. He has returned into battle, burning with desire and love for Me, even to the point of spilling his own blood.*

◆ This hadith, collected by the sage Abu Da'ud, was originally reported by the noble companion 'Abd-Allah ibn Mas'ud, may Allah be pleased with him.

Hadith ♦ *83*

THIS IS THE MOST SUBLIME OF DWELLINGS

Muhammad the Messenger, may Allah grant him perfect peace, once reported:

One of the people of Paradise will be brought forward, and Allah the Exalted will say: *O child of Adam, do you approve of the dwelling I have bestowed upon you?*

The blessed soul will reply: "O Lord, this is the most sublime of dwellings."

Bring forth the desires of your heart and make supplication to Me.

"I ask You to send me back to earth so that I can die ten times over in Your Way of love and self-sacrifice." The soul will make this request because of tasting in Paradise the unique Divine Blessing accorded to the martyrs.

♦ This hadith was collected by the sage an-Nasa'i from the transmission of the noble companion Anas, may Allah be pleased with him.

Hadith ◆ *84*

EVERY ONE OF THEM WILL BE BLESSED

The beloved Muhammad, may Allah grant him perfect peace, once revealed:

Allah has angels in constant search of persons who are practicing dhikr, the audible or inward repetition of the Divine Names. When one of them comes upon such a circle, intensely invoking and praising the Most High, this angel calls to the others: "Come to witness what you were divinely sent to witness." The angels surround the circle, wings extending into the heavens.

Their Lord, may He be glorified and magnified, asks them, even though His knowledge reaches infinitely beyond theirs: *What are My worshipers chanting?*

The angels reply: "They are exalting You, magnifying You, praising You, and glorifying You."

Do they see Me?

"No, our Lord, they do not see You."

What if they did see Me?

"If they saw You, they would intensify their worship of You, deepen their glorification of You, and increase their praise of You."

What are they asking of Me?

"They are asking for Paradise."

Have they seen it?

"No, O Lord, they have not seen it."

What if they did see it?

"If they saw Paradise, they would long for it with even greater ardor than before."

From what are they seeking refuge?

"From the Fire."

Have they seen it?

"No, O Lord, they have not seen it."

What if they saw it?

"If they saw the Fire, they would run even further from it, realizing its terrors even more completely."

O My angels, I take you as witnesses that I have forgiven the souls in this circle of remembrance.

An angel will say: "There is among them a certain one who is not truly part of them, entering their gathering for some other purpose."

The Lord will respond: *They are all the people of remembrance, and every one of them will be blessed.*

♦ This hadith, collected by the sage al-Bukhari, comes from the transmission of the intimate companion Abu Hurayra, may Allah be pleased with him.

Hadith ◆ 85

REPEAT *LA ILAHA ILALLAH* CEASELESSLY

The beloved Muhammad, may Allah grant him perfect peace, reported:

The Prophet Moses, peace be upon him, once supplicated: "O Lord, teach me a way by which I can continuously remember You and pray to You."

Repeat la ilaha ilallah, there is no Reality apart from Supreme Reality.

"O Lord, all your servants affirm this."

Repeat la ilaha ilallah ceaselessly.

"There is indeed no reality apart from You, O Allah, yet I long for an invocation that You would give uniquely to me."

My noble Moses, if the seven heavens and the seven levels of the earth, including all their inhabitants, were on one side of the scale and la ilaha ilallah on the other, la ilaha ilallah would have greater weight.

◆ This hadith, collected by the sage an-Nasa'i, comes from the transmission of the noble companion Abu Sa'id al-Khudri, may Allah be pleased with him.

Hadith ◆ 86

MEETING WITH THE ARCHANGEL

Muhammad the Messenger, may Allah bless and exalt him, once reported:

Archangel Gabriel came and announced: "O Muhammad, your Lord, may He be glorified, wishes to communicate these words to you: *Are you not pleased that each time someone invokes a blessing upon you, I offer that person divine blessing ten times over, and each time someone offers you a greeting of peace, I offer that person the blessing of ten greetings of peace?*"

◆ This hadith, collected by the sage an-Nasa'i, comes from the transmission of the noble companion Talha, may Allah be pleased with him, who recounted:

The Messenger of Allah, may Divine Peace be upon him, came to us one day with his countenance glowing. We said to him: "We see the happiness on your face." He told us then of meeting with the Archangel, the occurrence we have recorded here.

THE WOMB OF THE MOTHERS

Muhammad the Messenger, may Allah bestow blessing and peace upon him, once reported:

Allah Most High created the world, and when He had completed it, the womb of the mothers rose up and proclaimed: "I am the spiritual station of whoever seeks refuge in You from separation and division."

Allah responded: *Yes, you are this exalted station. I will unify Myself with those who are unified with you, and I will veil Myself from those who reject you. Are you content with My Decision?*

"Yes, I am fully content," mystic motherhood replied.

The Messenger of Allah, may Divine Peace be upon him, then commented:

Recite with sincerity these blessed words from the Holy Book if you wish to avoid separation and division: "Would anyone invested with genuine authority cause disorder on earth or sever the sacred ties of kinship? Those who act this way are chastened by Allah with spiritual deafness and blindness. Why do these persons fail to meditate on the Quranic teachings? Are there locks on their hearts?"

◆ This hadith, collected by the sage Muslim, comes from the transmission of the intimate companion Abu Hurayra, may Allah be pleased with him.

Hadith ◆ 88

MY LOVE BELONGS TO THOSE WHO LOVE

The beloved Muhammad, may Allah bestow peace upon him, once reported these words directly from the Most High:

My love belongs to those who love each other in Me, who experience intimacy in Me, who shower each other with goodness for My Sake, and who visit each other joyfully for My Sake.

◆ This hadith, collected by the sage Malik ibn Anas, comes from the transmission of the noble companion Mu'adh, may Allah be pleased with him.

Hadith ◆ 89

YOU LOVE MY SERVANT, TOO

The beloved Muhammad, may Allah bestow peace and blessing upon him, once reported:

When Allah deeply loves one of His servants, He calls Gabriel and informs the Archangel: *I love this person; you love My servant, too.*

From that moment, Gabriel loves this person and announces throughout the heavens: "Allah Most High loves this person; you love this servant, too." From that moment, the inhabitants of the heavens love this person. Afterward, this servant begins to be loved and recognized widely by those on earth.

When Allah withdraws His Good Pleasure from one of His servants, He summons Gabriel and informs the Archangel: *I am displeased with this person; you be displeased with this unfaithful servant, too.*

From that moment, Gabriel feels displeased with this person and announces to the inhabitants of the heavens: "Allah Most High has withdrawn His Good Pleasure from this person; you be displeased, too." From that moment, they become displeased. Afterward, this servant begins to encounter widespread displeasure from those on earth.

◆ This hadith, collected by the sage Muslim, comes from the transmission of the intimate companion Abu Hurayra, may Allah be pleased with him.

Hadith ◆ 90

I HAVE ALREADY FORGIVEN YOU

A servant commits a transgression and prays: "O my Lord, forgive this transgression."

The Most High responds:

My servant has committed a transgression yet knows that I am the Lord who forgives and erases transgressions.

This servant again falls into error and prays: "O my Lord, forgive this error."

Allah, may He be glorified, proclaims:

My servant has fallen into error but knows that I am the Lord who forgives and erases error.

This servant again transgresses and prays: "O my Lord, forgive me."

Allah the Compassionate and Merciful responds:

My servant has transgressed yet knows that I am the Lord who forgives and erases transgression. Do whatever you wish, My truly faithful servant, for I have already forgiven you.

◆ This hadith, collected by the sage Muslim, comes from the transmission of the intimate companion Abu Hurayra, may Allah be pleased with him.

Hadith ◆ 91

I AM THE HEARING BY WHICH THEY HEAR

Muhammad the Messenger, may Allah bestow peace upon him, once reported these words directly from the Most High:

Whoever acts with hostility toward one of My intimate servants, upon this aggressor I declare war. Human beings cannot approach Me by any way dearer to Me than performing what I have commanded. And My intimate servants never cease to come nearer and nearer to Me through performing acts of loving worship beyond what I have commanded until I embrace them entirely in My Love. When I embrace them, I am the hearing by which they hear, the seeing by which they see, the hands with which they grasp, and the feet with which they walk. If they supplicate Me for all humanity, certainly I will respond. If they seek refuge with Me for all humanity, surely I will grant it. None of My Divine Actions causes Me greater empathy than to withdraw from the earthly body the eternal soul of a believer who abhors death. It actually causes Me Divine Distress to afflict one of My lovers in this way.

◆ This hadith, collected by the sage al-Bukhari, comes from the transmission of the intimate companion Abu Hurayra, may Allah be pleased with him.

Hadith ◆ 92

THE DESIRE TO BEHOLD MY FACE

The beloved Muhammad, may Divine Peace and Blessings be upon him, once reported:

On the Day of Resurrection, the sealed books of the souls will be brought before Allah Most High and opened. The Exalted and Glorious One will instruct the angels: *Reject those particular actions and accept only these.*

The angels will reply: "We swear by Your Divine Power that we see only good in those actions that You command us to reject."

The Most High, who is infinitely more knowing than they, will answer: *These deeds were performed for other purposes than the longing to please only Me. Today, I will accept only those good actions that spring from the desire to behold My Face.*

◆ This hadith, collected by the sage ad-Daraqutri, comes from the transmission of the noble companion Anas ibn Malik, may Allah be pleased with him.

Hadith ◆ 93

THOSE WHO ARE IN MY SERVICE

The beloved Muhammad, may Divine Peace be upon him, reported these words directly from Allah Most High:

O physical world, serve those who are in My Service. O physical world, obstruct those who serve only you.

◆ This hadith, collected by the sage ʿAbd-al-Haqq, comes from the transmission of the noble companion ʿAbd-Allah ibn Masʿud, may Allah be pleased with him.

Hadith ◆ 94

THOSE WHO HAVE REJECTED ME

The Exalted and Glorious One proclaims:

Those servants to whom I grant health and ease of life and who enjoy these for five whole years without once turning to Me in thankfulness are those who have rejected Me.

◆ This hadith, collected by the sage Abu Bakr ibn Abi Shayba, comes from the transmission of the noble companion Abu Sa'id al-Khudri, may Allah be pleased with him.

Hadith ✦ 95

THE DIVINE NAME

The beloved Muhammad, may Divine Peace be upon him, once reported:

On the Day of Resurrection, the Most High will extend His Mercy upon a member of my community whose errors surpass those of other created beings. Allah will unroll before this soul ninety-nine scrolls documenting its wrong actions, each scroll reaching as far as the eye can see. Then Allah will question: *Do you contest anything recorded here? Have the angels who witnessed your deeds been unjust to you?*

"No, my Lord."

Do you have any argument to bring in your favor?

"No, my Lord."

Yet you have a single good deed that is cherished by the Divine Presence. This Day, no chastisement will touch you.

A small page will then be brought forth, on which is inscribed: "I witness that there is no reality apart from the One Reality, Allah Most High, and I witness that Muhammad is His Servant and Messenger."

Allah will command: *Come close, O My servant, and weigh this page on the Balance of Truth.*

The soul will inquire: "My Lord, what weight has this small page compared to those extensive scrolls?"

Allah will assure the soul: *You will not be treated unfairly.*

Thereupon, the scrolls will be placed on one side of the vast scale, the single sheet of paper on the other. The ninety-nine scrolls will be light, and the small page will weigh heavily. Nothing has true weight or substance other than the Divine Name.

♦ This hadith, collected by the sage at-Tirmidhi, comes from the transmission of the noble companion 'Abd-Allah ibn 'Amru ibn al-'As, may Allah be pleased with him.

THE NATURE OF ANGELS

The beloved Muhammad, may Divine Peace be upon him, once clarified the nature of angels:

They stand before the Most High and testify on behalf of souls who have performed pious actions. Allah addresses His angels: *You are only the recorders of the actions of My servants, but I am the Discerning One who knows what is in their secret hearts. This particular soul whom you consider pious was not truly seeking Me through these devotional deeds but something other than Me. My Displeasure is upon this soul.*

◆ This hadith, collected by the sage Ibn al-Mubarak, comes from the transmission of the companion Mu'adh ibn Jabal, may Allah be pleased with him.

Hadith ◆ 97

I PROMISE TO HELP YOU

The beloved Muhammad, may Allah shower peace upon him, once revealed:

There are three supplicants whose prayers are assured: the one who is fasting for the sake of Allah, as long as the fast is not broken; the leader of prayers who remains fair to all persons; and the innocent victim. Allah will elevate them above the seven heavens and will open before them the Gates of Paradise. The Lord, glorified be He, proclaims to these supplicants: *By My Own Divine Power, I promise to help you when the time is ripe.*

◆ This hadith, collected by the sage at-Tirmidhi, comes from the transmission of the intimate companion Abu Hurayra, may Allah be pleased with him.

Hadith ♦ *98*

YOU WOULD HAVE FOUND ME

Allah the Exalted and Majestic will proclaim on the Day of Resurrection:

O children of Adam, I was sick and you did not visit Me.

The souls will respond: "O Lord, how could we visit You, who are the Lord of all the Worlds?" Allah will answer:

Were you not aware that My servants known to you fell sick and you did not visit them? Are you not aware that if you had visited them you would have found Me through them?

O children of Adam, I asked you for food and you did not feed Me.

The souls will respond: "O Lord, how could we feed You, who are the Lord of all the Worlds?" Allah will answer:

Were you not aware that My servants known to you asked for food and you did not feed them? Are you not aware that if you had fed them you would have found Me through this offering?

O children of Adam, I asked you for drink and you did not quench My thirst.

The souls will respond: "O Lord, how could we quench the thirst of the Lord of all the Worlds?" Allah will answer:

My servants known to you asked you for drink, and you did not provide it for them. If you had quenched their thirst, you would have found Me through this offering.

◆ This hadith, collected by the sage Muslim, comes from the transmission of the intimate companion Abu Hurayra, may Allah be pleased with him.

Hadith ♦ 99

YOU HAVE LIED

The beloved Messenger, may Allah bestow blessing and peace upon him, once reported:

> When the Day of Resurrection arrives, Allah Most High will descend to the servants in order to evaluate them. The members of each spiritual community will be kneeling in submission. The first servant to be called forth from humanity will be one who knows the entire Quran by heart, then one martyred in the way of Allah, then someone of abundant wealth. Allah will address the reciter of Quran: *Did I not teach you what I originally transmitted to the heart of My Messenger?*
>
> "Yes, O Lord."
>
> *Did you act according to the knowledge given you?*
>
> "I devoted myself night and day to its recitation."
>
> Allah will reply, *You have lied,* and the angels will confirm: "You have lied."
>
> Allah Most High will reveal: *You cared above all that people would say, "This person is a reciter of Quran." In fact, that was said, and that alone will be your reward.*

The wealthy one will then be brought forward. Allah will inquire: *Did I not generously endow you so that you did not have to ask favors from anyone?*

"Yes, O Lord."

What did you do with what I gave you?

"I strengthened the bonds of kinship and gave in charity."

Allah will then proclaim, *You have lied,* and the angels will confirm: "You have lied."

Allah Most High will reveal: *You cared above all that people would say, "This person is supremely generous." In fact, that was said, and that alone will be your reward.*

Then the martyr in the way of Allah will be brought forward and Allah will address this soul: *On what occasion were you martyred?*

"O Lord, You commanded Holy Warfare and I died for Your Cause."

Allah Most High will then proclaim, *You have lied,* and the angels will confirm: "You have lied."

Allah Most High will reveal: *You cared above all that people would say, "This person is supremely courageous." In fact, that was said, and that alone will be your reward.*

Muhammad the Messenger, may Allah grant him peace, then struck my knee with his palm and said: "O Abu Hurayra, these three will be the first to encounter the Fire on the Day of Resurrection."

♦ This hadith, collected by the sage at-Tirmidhi, comes from the transmission of the intimate companion Abu Hurayra, may Allah be pleased with him.

Hadith ◆ 100

THE FINAL DAY

The beloved Messenger, may Allah bestow peace upon him, once witnessed:

By the One who holds my very soul in His Hand, you will have no more difficulty seeing your Lord on the Final Day than seeing the radiant sun or the full moon in a clear sky.

Allah Most High will seek out His servant on that Day and inquire: *O My servant, was I not generous toward you? Have I not given you a loving companion in life? Have I not provided horses and camels for you? Have I not made you a leader and appointed for you one-fourth of the abundance of conquest?*

"Lord, You have done all this."

Were you consciously preparing yourself for meeting Me?

"No, O Lord, I was not."

I will now veil you from My Presence for as long as you have turned away from Me.

Then Allah Most High will seek out another servant, find this soul also unprepared, and proclaim: *I will now veil you from My Presence for as long as you have turned away from Me.*

Then the Most High will seek out and question a third servant in the same way. The soul will reply: "O Lord, I believed in You and Your Books and Your Messengers. I prayed, I fasted, and I gave in charity." This servant will praise Allah with traditional praises.

Inquiring, *Are these your true feelings?* the Lord will announce to that servant: *We will send Our witnesses to testify concerning you.* The soul will consider inwardly, "Who could testify against me?" His lips will then be sealed, and to his limbs, flesh, and bones Allah will declare: *Speak!* These witnesses will reveal all the unkind, selfish actions of this person and will refute the empty claims of the soul. Such is the destiny of the hypocrites, who bring down Divine Chastening upon themselves.

◆ This hadith, collected by the sage Muslim, comes from the transmission of the intimate companion Abu Hurayra, may Allah be pleased with him.

Hadith ◆ *101*

IN THE GARDEN OF PARADISE

The beloved Muhammad, may Allah bestow Divine Peace upon him, once expressed to the sublime companion 'Ali these words, which were then transmitted, through many faultless witnesses, to the present poor lover, Ibn al Arabi, while seated with his mystic guide before the noble Ka'ba in the Masjid al Haraam:

In the Garden of Paradise, Allah Most High will communicate to the people of Paradise: *I am Allah the Generous, the Self-Sufficient, the Integral, the Truthful. This is My Abode, where I have now established you. This is My Paradise, which I have now opened for you. And here is My Own Self, which I now reveal to you. Here is My Hand, which distributes the dew and the rain, now open and extended over you. I will never draw it back from you. I now gaze at you, and My direct gaze will never turn away from you. Ask Me what you wish and what you ardently desire, for I have made you intimate with My Own Self. I am your Friend and your Confidant. There will never again exist for you need or privation, tribulation or misery, neither weakness nor aging, neither anger nor constraint nor adversity. The delights of eternity now surround you. You are the ones who are secure, who are eternally abiding, the noble ones, the ones who ceaselessly receive My Generosity. You are the distinguished royal souls who obeyed Me and followed My*

Guidance. Ask of Me, and I will satisfy you completely from My Abundance.

The chosen ones will then cry out: "Our Lord, the delights of Paradise are neither what we hope for nor desire. What we ardently long for is You alone, the timeless vision of Your Noble Blessed Countenance and Your Good Pleasure upon us eternally."

Whereupon the Supreme One, the All-Sublime, the Sultan of the Divine Kingdom, the All-Generous Giver, may He be glorified and exalted, will respond to them: *Here is My Countenance, revealing Itself to you forever. Therefore rejoice, for My Own Self is pleased with you. Rejoice! Turn to your companions, O My chosen ones. Embrace them and celebrate together the mystical marriage. Turn to the other souls linked to you, and share your joy. Go to your elevated spiritual stations and enter them joyfully. Go to your interior gardens and stroll there. Go to your heavenly mounts and ride them. Recline on your couches of rich brocade. Experience intimacy with your companions in the inner chambers. Go to the gifts that are destined to you from your Lord, and gratefully receive them. Don your robes of Paradise. Attend your spiritual gatherings and converse with each other in love and praise. Without entering sleep or losing consciousness, repose beneath deep shade in the most peaceful refuge, nearness to the All-Majestic One. Visit the holy waters of Paradise: the upwelling spring of Kawthar; the fragrant spring of Kafur, where servants of Allah drink ecstatically; the spring of Clarity; the resonant fountain of Tasnim, where souls of nearness drink; the healing springs of Salsabil and Zanjabil. Immerse yourselves in these waters and quench your spiritual thirst with them. This will be the bliss of union, the height of mystical return.*

Thereupon, recline on green cushions and rich carpets placed on raised couches in expansive shade, where water gushes forth and fruits of wisdom abound, unrestricted and inexhaustible.

The Messenger of Allah, may peace be upon him, concluded this account with words from the Glorious Quran: "The companions of Paradise will be absorbed in bliss on this Day—they and their noble spouses, resting upon divans in cool shade. There will be manifest for them fruits of wisdom and all they can desire, contained in the Word from their Most Loving Lord: *Peace be upon you.*" Once again the beloved Muhammad, may peace be upon him, chanted from the Book of Reality: "The lovers in Paradise experience this eternal Day as permanent repose, the most beautiful spiritual station, Peace."

◆ This hadith was imparted to me by the Shaykh, the Imam, the Honored, the entrusted keeper of Hadith, Abu Muhammad Yunus ibn Yahya. We recited it mutually to each other several times, alternately speaking and listening, in the precincts of the Haram ash-Sharif, facing the Ka'ba, in the month of Jumada al-Akhira in the year 599.

THIS BOOK, called *Mishkat al-Anwar*, composed of the divine transmissions from Allah Most High, has now been completed with its third part in the holy precincts of the Ka'ba at midday, Sunday, the last day of the month of Jumada al-Akhira, in the year 599. It was inscribed by the hand of its author, Muhammad ibn 'Ali Ibn Muhammad Ibn al-'Arabi at-Ta'i al-Hatimi. May Allah extend His Mercy upon the one who reads this book and offers prayer for its author, and may Allah send his blessings and grace upon our Master Muhammad, upon his pure family and upon all his noble companions throughout time.

O You in Whom I place my trust and my hope,
Seal all my actions with Goodness.